I want to tell you about my baby.

a book by
Roslyn Banish

Wingbow Press, Berkeley

To Andrew Wolf Epstein

Very special thanks to the Flack Family: Betsy and Jim,
Andrew and Bardin, and Betsy's parents, Beulah and
Fran Hodge.

The medical photographs were assisted by Christa
Williams R.N., Director, FAMCAP, Leon Zdan, M.D.,
Richard Topel, M.D., all of Kaiser-Permanente Medical
Center, San Francisco. The photograph on page 13 was
done by Dirk Schenkkan.

Wingbow Press books are published and distributed
by Bookpeople, 2929 Fifth Street, Berkeley,
California 94710

Designed by Michael Patrick Cronan

Library of Congress Cataloging in Publication Data
Banish, Roslyn, 1942–
    I want to tell you about my baby.

Summary: A little boy explains his mother's pregnancy
and childbirth, the care the newborn needs, and his feelings
about his baby brother.
    1. Infants—Juvenile literature. 2. Brothers and sisters—
Juvenile literature. [1. Pregnancy, 2. Childbirth. 3. Babies.
4. Brothers and sisters] I. Title.
HQ774.B32   306.8'7   81-16489
ISBN 0-914728-35-0 (pbk.)   AACR2

First Printing January 1982
Second Printing May 1983
Third Printing September 1985

I want to
tell you
about my
baby.

That's my Mom and Dad and me.
The baby is growing inside my Mom.
We have bread to feed the ducks.

My Dad holds me upside down. I love it.
My Mom can't pick me up anymore.
The baby is too big.
She can't even button her jacket.

Mom is reading a story to me.
I can't sit on her lap anymore.
She is too bumpy.
I want her to have a lap.

That's me talking to the baby. "Hi, Baby." The baby doesn't answer. I don't like waiting for the baby.

My Mom lets me touch her big belly.
Sometimes I feel the baby move. It feels funny.
My Mom says the baby gets bigger every day.

I go to the doctor with
my Mom. He listens to
the baby's heart beat
with a special radio.
The doctor says we
have to wait some more
before the baby is born.

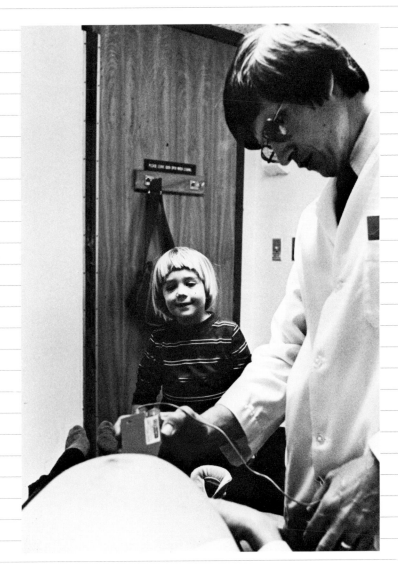

My Mom is tired all the time.
The baby makes her sleepy.
I want her to play with me like she used to.

I look at a book all by myself. It's about ships.
I love ships and dinosaurs and spaceships and
Batman and Superman and oatmeal cookies with raisins.

We're doing exercises. I am wearing my Superman tights.
My Mom has to get strong so she can push the baby out.
I am strong because I am Superman.

My Dad and I are getting the baby's room ready. He tells me this little bed was mine when I was a baby. Now I am a big boy. I have a BIG bed.

I don't remember when I was a baby.
My Dad shows me my baby pictures.
Boy, do I look funny!

This is me when I was a baby.

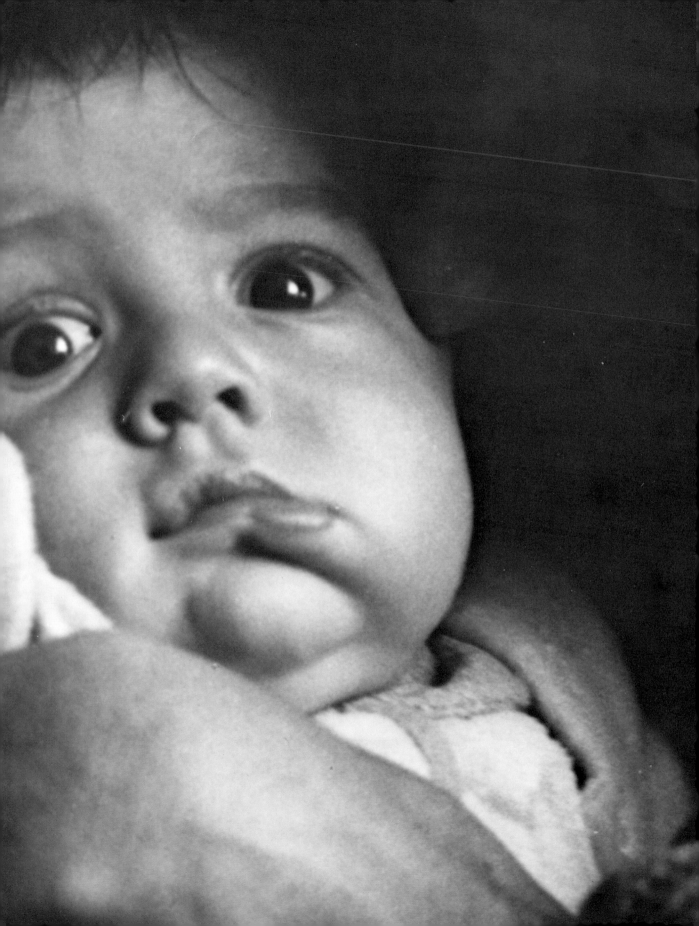

That's my Grandma and Grandpa.
They are going to take care of me when the
baby comes. They like to give me presents.

One day my Mom tells me the baby is ready to be born. Hooray! No more waiting. My Mom and Dad go to the hospital.

. . . and I stay home with my Grandma and Grandpa. We make oatmeal cookies with raisins. When will my Mom come home?

Grandma sews an "S" on my Superman cape.

I think about Superman and my Mom.

My Mom is in this hospital.

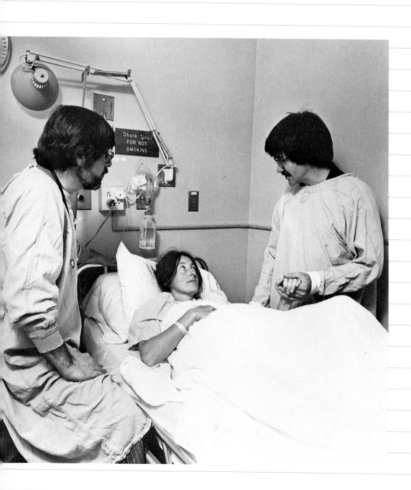

Here she is waiting for
the baby to be born.
The man with my Dad
is the doctor. He is
going to help my Mom.

My Mom gives a big push. The baby comes out an opening between her legs. The doctor catches it and says it's a boy. My Dad says that is how I was born too.

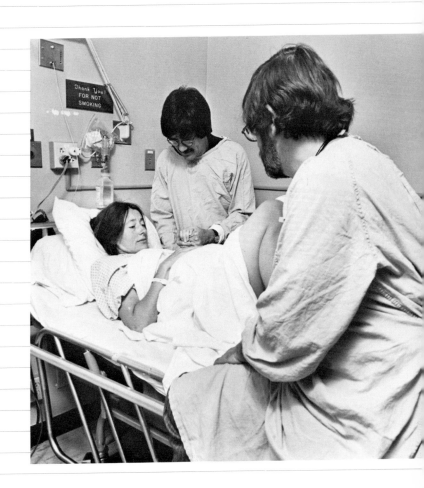

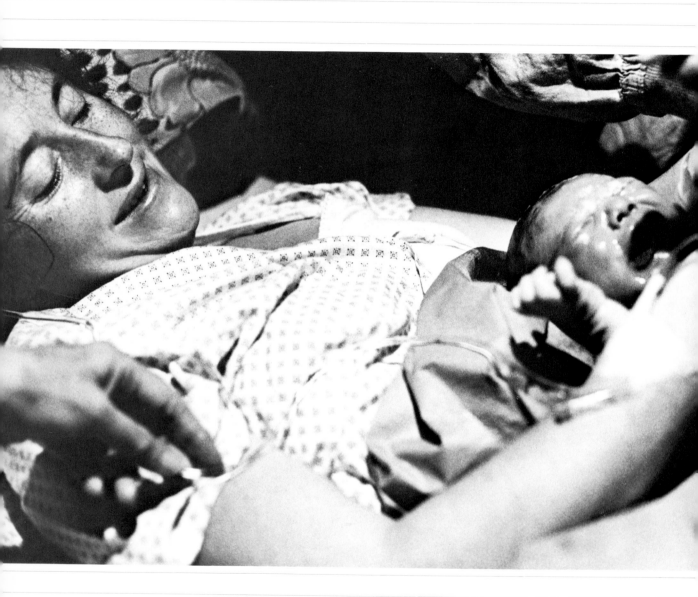

That means I have a brother.

Then they give him a big hug.

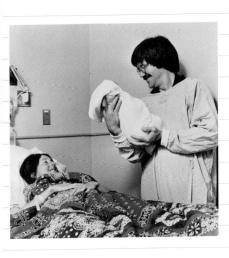

They wrap up the baby
to keep him warm.

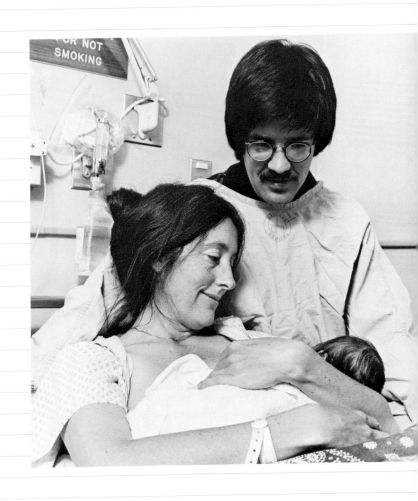

My Grandpa takes me to the hospital.
Here I'm waiting to see the baby.
Where is my Mom?
Where is the baby?

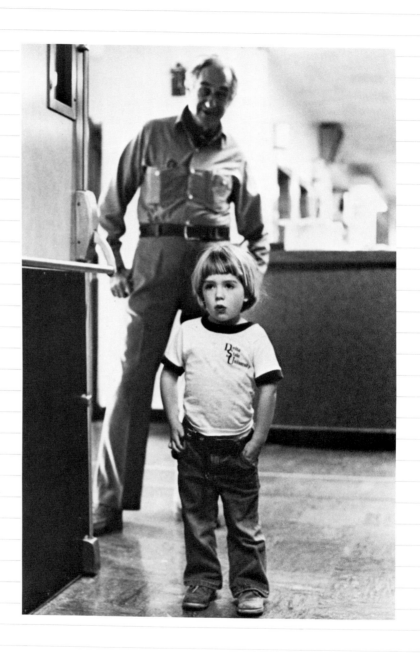

Here she is!
My Mom gives me a great big hug
and says "I love you."
I tell her to come home.

My Dad shows the baby to me.

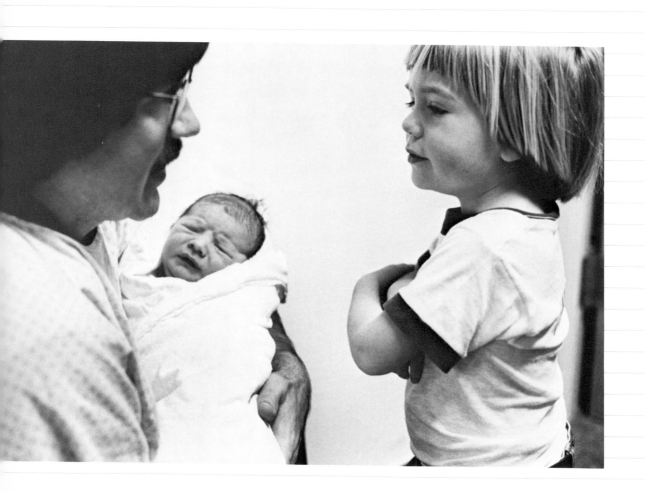

He is so little and has lots of wrinkles.

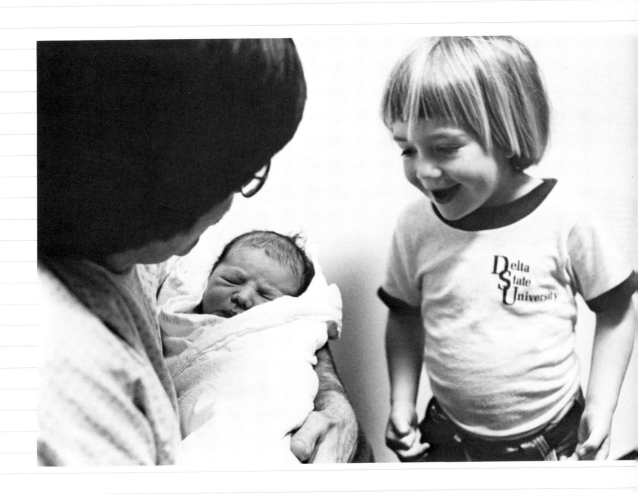

My Mom and the baby stay in the hospital to rest.
Then my Dad goes to pick them up.
A nurse carries the baby to the car.

My Mom and the baby come home.

. . . and look at the baby.

I fly to my Dad . . .

The baby is home now but I can't
play with him.
He just wants to sleep. . . .

. . . and cry

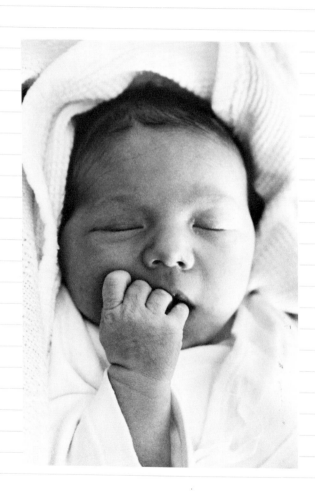

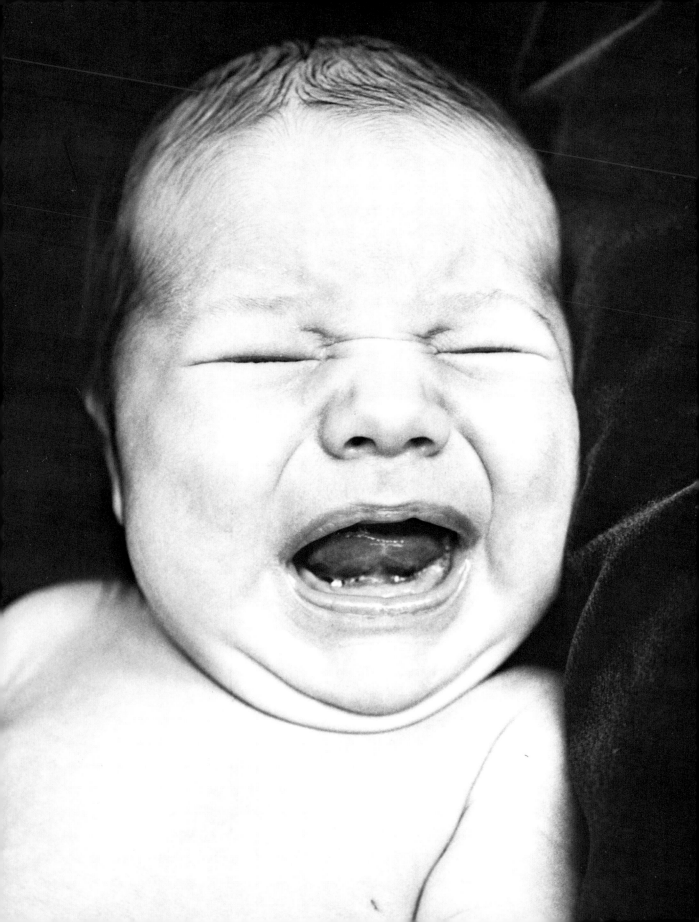

. . . and eat.
Here he gets milk from my Mom's breast.

. . . and eat some more.
My Dad gives him a bottle sometimes.

My Mom lets me help with the baby's first bath.
He likes it because I am gentle.

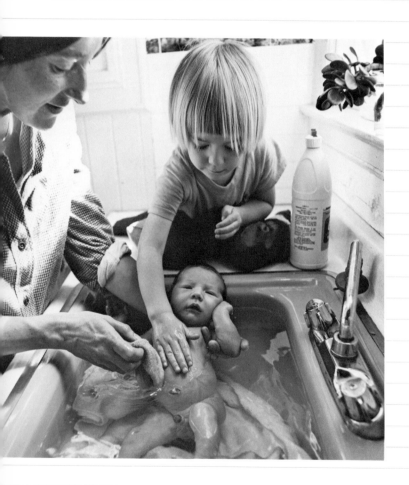

I have to be quiet all the time so I don't wake the baby.
That's my Mom looking like an old meany.
It's not so much fun having a baby in the family.

My Mom has to hold him a lot so he will be happy.
I want her to hold me so I will be happy too.

The baby gets all the presents. I get to open them.
There is nothing fun for me to play with.

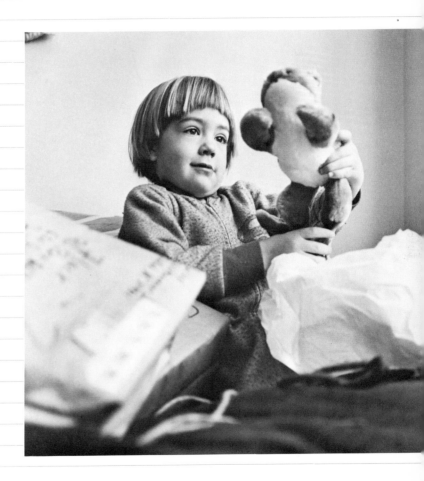

There he is nursing again.
I want my Mom to play with me NOW.

That's me crying. I'm crying because I'm mad. I don't like the baby.

That's the baby crying. He's crying because that's what little babies do.

My Mom says she loves me very, very much and that she can hug us both—even at the same time.

And my Dad tells me
he loves me very, very much—
and that even though we have
a baby, we can still play and
roughhouse and hang upside
down.

41

One day my Baby smiles at me.   I feel happy.

We play in my room. I show him my toys.
Someday he will be a good friend.
That's what my Mom and Dad tell me.
I think he likes me already.

My friends at school want a baby just like mine.
I tell them they can't have him.

That's my Mom and Dad and me.
My baby is in the stroller.
We have bread to feed the ducks.
There you are, ducks!

My thanks to Christa Williams R.N., Director, FAMCAP,
Leon Zdan, M.D., Richard Topel, M.D., all of
Kaiser-Permanente Medical Center, San Francisco,
for assisting with the medical photographs and
Dirk Schenkkan for the photograph on page 13.